SONORAN DESERT FROG

WRITTEN & ILLUSTRATED BY

LYNN ZUBAL

To order additional copies of this book, contact:
Xlibris
844-714-8691
www.Xlibris.com
Orders@Xlibris.com

ISBN: Softcover   978-1-6641-2500-1
         EBook   978-1-6641-2499-8

Print information available on the last page

Rev. date: 08/24/2020

Sonoran
Desert Frog

Written and
Illustrated by

LYNN ZUBAL

Most of the year
the Sonoran frog
sleeps underground.

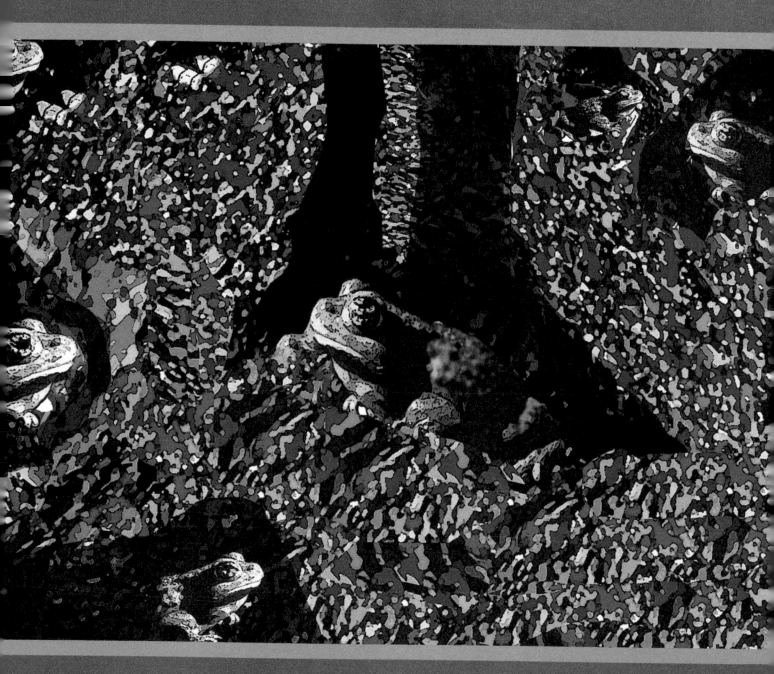

When the first monsoon rain arrives the Sonoran frog awakens and comes to the desert surface.

The time is usually May through September.

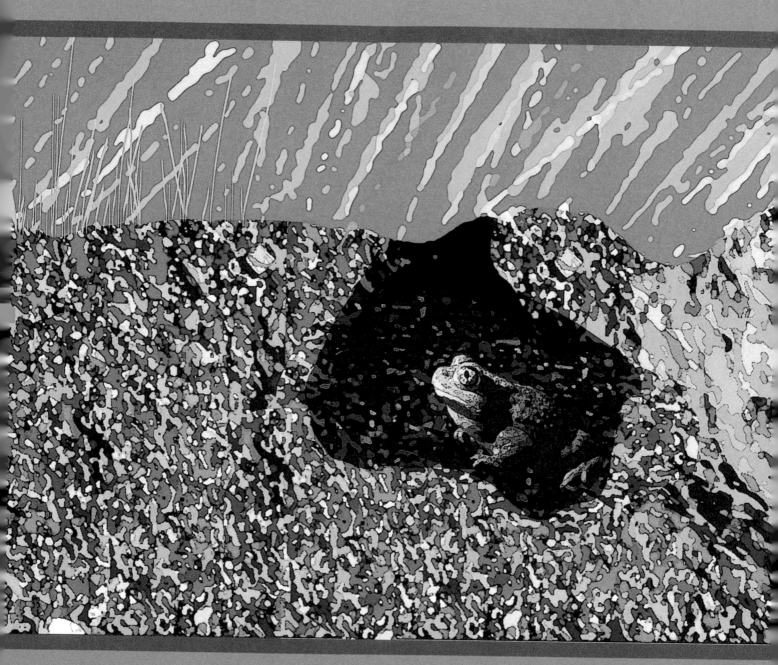

Monarch butterflies come out after the monsoon rain to welcome the Sonoran frog.

The scorpions come out during the monsoon season.

The dragonflies come out
during the monsoon rain.
Dragonflies love water.

Tarantulas come out during the monsoon rain.

The male's mating call is weak, sounding somewhat like a ferryboat whistle. Once the females agree on a mate, the mating begins.

Eggs are laid in temporary rainpools and permanent ponds. Larvae change after 6 to 10 weeks.

After 6 to 10 weeks the Sonoran frogs return to the underground. This species lives at least 10 years, and perhaps as many as 20 years.

Printed in the United States
By Bookmasters